Remember Who You Are

-The Story Behind the Song-

T0272331

Remember Who You Are

- The Story Behind the Song -

Angelica Ganea-Mileto

Stream Entertainment

Stream Entertainment, Inc.
Toronto, Canada,
URL: www.StreamEntertainment.ca
E-mail: mail@StreamEntertainment.ca

First printing 2010
ISBN 978-0-9784940-0-1 paperback
Printed in Canada

Book layout: Ellen Mann
Photography: Maylynn Quan

Cover design: Angelica
URL: www.iamAngelica.com

Dedication

I dedicate my book to the angel who gave me the confidence that I was undeniably on the right path, and that all the frustrations and unwanted feelings I was experiencing came from the dichotomy of knowing deep within who I am, but not allowing myself to be that. Through his beautiful innocence, this angel reminded me that the desire I carved out so precisely as a child is shining now more vibrantly than ever, so ready to show me how being fulfilled feels— in real life, this time.

With endless love and appreciation,
To Pino, my husband, my angel.

Acknowledgments

It is with much appreciation that I would like to acknowledge two very important people who helped me finalize my manuscript:

Angela Wingfield for her impeccable professional approach to this project and her skillful and precise editing of every detail.

Ellen Mann for the creative expression reflected in the layout and proofreading. She approached my project with loving, unconditional support and treated it as her own.

Special thanks

There is a place where the truth resides and calls out to us. It is that one place where we will always find comfort. It is where we find the courage and inspiration to make the right choices and move forward and accomplish what we desire. No pretense, no lies, no guilt, no broken promises or disappointments can ever spring forth from it. It is the place of The Absolute— the Inner Self.

Even though every single one of us is held within that heavenly state (and therefore we all can recognize at some level what the truth is), it has taken humanity many, many years to come to the point of beginning to be open to what is almost common knowledge today: that we are not separate from God— Truth, and therefore we are worthy and beautiful, and the creators of our own reality.

We now know this primarily because of the great teachers who held onto the Vision and made the journey to bring this ancient knowledge to the attention of us all. They have made is so much easier for me to become more aware of the truth within. Reading their work gives me peace and a feeling of deep appreciation— I finally understand my own words. What I have been feeling and writing about all of these years has been confirmed. Now I have found the confidence to bring forth my own perspective.

With a heart full of gratitude I would like to acknowledge the teachers whom I have been so very blessed to meet in person, and also those whom I have never met but whose writings have greatly influenced me. My deepest love goes to all who are encouraging the rest of us to take the most rewarding journey of our lives: the journey to rediscover our own divinity, identity, and beauty:

Dr. Kenneth George Mills, philosopher, conductor, composer, poet, artist, lecturer— my dear mentor who taught me the importance of holding onto my true identity. His genuine smile at the sound of my voice still shines before me, and his words of true elevation still echo in my head: ". . . and you haven't even scratched the surface yet, Angelica."

Giovanni (John) Ruicci— my dear friend and mentor, one of the most compassionate, trustworthy, and patient people I have ever met, and the first to bring to my attention the simple, yet powerful, "You decide."

"A Course in Miracles" published by the Foundation for Inner Peace which has been a guiding light for me, from which comes this quote: "I understand that miracles are natural because they are expressions of love."

Bob Proctor, Neale D. Walsch, Eckhart Tolle, Rhonda Byrne, Esther and Jerry Hicks (Abraham-Hicks), and so many others whose work inspire one to find the peace within— the only way to bring peace to the world.

Contents

About Angelica
(pronounced AHN-JE-LEE-KAH)

While watching Angelica perform, one could say very easily and without reservation that she is a one-of-a-kind performer. One might wonder, how does she allow herself to surrender to her passion with such abandon? How does she arrive at a point where she emanates through every breath, through every sound and gesture she makes, so much power, confidence, strength and vulnerability, but most of all, so much love for what she does?

This is Angelica Ganea-Mileto, a singer, songwriter and author, and this is the story behind her journey through life...

Angelica's roots lie in the shores of the Blue Danube in Romania in the town of Galati. The eldest of three children in a middle-class family, Angelica has fond memories of the moments she shared with her siblings and friends, putting shows together for the people in the neighborhood. Her father, from whom she inherited her beautiful voice, always encouraged his three children to sing their hearts out. Despite the constraints and hardships of a communist environment, Angelica, under her parents' love and care, intuitively followed her heart by doing what she loved most.

Angelica's stage experience started when she was only five years old with music and dance as the main focus of her childhood days. While performing in one of her Kindergarten recitals, Rusalim Vlaicu, a nationally known ballet coach from the School of Arts spotted this aspiring little girl dancing passionately in the front line. He was scouting for young talented children to attend his school and after the performance he approached Angelica's parents. Without hesitation they enrolled her in the School of Arts and Angelica began her study of the art of ballet.

It wasn't long before Gheorghe Dragomir, the vocal teacher in charge of the music department at the school recognized the kindness and sincerity conveyed by the tone of Angelica's voice. He notified her parents and said that he felt Angelica should also join the School of Arts' orchestra— as a soloist. That was one of the most important steps for Angelica for it was the beginning of the instruction that helped mold her into the confident performer she is today. Only eight years old, Angelica was already "at home" on stage performing live, while accompanied by a large orchestra and back-up singers. Her artistic talent and potential shone through all of her performances, causing those in the audience to often remark, "There is something special about the tone of her voice."

Many professionals in charge of guiding children on their artistic path wanted to work with Angelica. Angelica, now six years old, was asked by Mrs. Ioan Aurelia, the leader of a large children's choir, to join them. Performing with the choir had an important impact on the future of her vocal career as it helped her develop a keen ear for sound and harmonies. Angelica sang with the choir for eight years, competing yearly on a national level against other children's choirs. It was during her last year as a member of the choir that the teacher decided to change the pace and have the choir compete this time by performing a song that involved two soloists. At fourteen years old Angelica had the honor of being chosen to be the lead soprano singer. That year, their performance won first place in the national competition "Songs for Romania" (Cantarea Romaniei").

Being part of the prestigious School of Arts, participating in both ballet and music full time made Angelica a busy child. Sometimes she would wake up at four in the morning to do her school homework because she didn't want to take time away from her late afternoon and evening practice. On weekends, she sang and danced in live shows, which took place at various theatres across the city. She soon became a popular performer in her hometown.

During these years other creative talents began to develop in Angelica. She became very interested in fashion and even created her own outfits to wear on stage. Her unique style caught the attention of a fashion designer working for "The Fashion House Galati" who, after seeing her perform, asked Angelica to work as a designer for the firm. Angelica was sixteen years old at the time and wisely did not mention to the designer that the very dress she had just worn on stage was made from the burgundy velvet curtains in her home. Although shocked at seeing her beautiful burgundy velvet curtains gone, Angelica's mother never made it an issue. Instead, with a heart full of appreciation for such a creative being, she proudly watched her daughter bring to life beautiful and unique outfits out of their very limited resources.

Then there were no craft stores and no places to go buy any of the supplies that are found in abundance today. Even sequins were hard to find. In order for Angelica to finish a bustier, she collected sequins from her friends' mother's old dresses. In order to match her shoes with her dresses, she would paint them with the only silver paint she could find: a heavy duty paint that her grandmother used to paint her wood burning stove. There was no such thing as *impossible* in Angelica's world. Every time she would get an idea, her first and only thought was, "How can I make this work?" And she would always find a way.

After years of seeing her lead such an active and busy life, Angelica's parents encouraged her to slow down because they were worried she might become overwhelmed. However, her rebellious, straightforward answer made her parents realize that Angelica was serious about her regular practice. It was not kid's play for her. It was what she wanted and who she was. So her mother and father continued to support her fully, giving her all the love and encouragement she needed.

At the age of nineteen, there was a breakthrough in Angelica's career. Her attention was caught by a singing competition that was being organized and broadcast nationwide by National Television, the only TV station in Romania at the time (Toamna Muzicala Bacauana"). She decided to go to the audition, and it turned out to be quite unique experience. After having performed a late show followed by a wedding, which traditionally in Romania doesn't end until the next morning, Angelica took the early morning train to the audition. Unfortunately she fell asleep and missed her stop and didn't arrive until after the auditions had finished. The jury had already chosen the twenty finalists and was preparing to announce the winning contestants.

All participants were anxiously waiting for the results

when Angelica, modestly dressed (the 'girl next-door' look) knocked at the door and asked, "Could you please let me sing for you? Just for one minute. I have come from four hours away, and I missed my stop." Titus Munteanu, the top TV producer in the country at the time, looked at her. He seemed puzzled by Angelica's straightforward, innocent look and then said, "OK. Let's hear you. Do you have a score for your song?" She pulled out a wrinkled paper from her pocket and handed it to the pianist. They allowed her to sing the entire song. At the end, the producer of the show invited her to sit down. He did not have to ask the other members of the jury if they considered her a participant; the look on their faces said it all. Angelica's name was at the top of the list ten seconds after she had sung for them!

Angelica went on to win the Trophy of the competition and received instant recognition as one of the most talented rising stars. It was not long before some of Romania's top songwriters, including Ion Cristinoiu, Marius Teicu, Vasile Veselovschi began showing interest in working with her. Soon she was performing in live TV shows and touring the country.

As Angelica was also a strong advocate of continuous growth and development, she decided to go to university and enrolled in the Music Hall program in Bucharest, the capital of Romania. It was during her first year at the university that she got a job at Constantin Tanase Theatre in Bucharest, the most prestigious musical theatre in the city. She performed with many of the country's most acclaimed singers and actors including Alexandru Arsinel and Stela Popescu.

One day, as she was walking in the hallway of the university, she heard a beautiful perfect sound coming from one of the classrooms. She approached the door and listened. It was an opera class, one of the many programs the university was offering. She loved that sound and instantly thought to herself, "I would love to be able to sing like that." She waited for the class to end and opened the door. Mr. Baiasu, the professor in charge of the opera class, asked her quietly, "Can I help you?" "I would really love it if you would allow me to try that song …" Angelica said. He smiled softly and handed her the music score.

Ever since she was a little girl, Angelica had the ability to alter her voice and mimic different singers, even instruments. Opera was no different for her. Recalling the sound she had just heard, she opened her mouth and started singing. The professor was astonished at what he heard. He could not believe it when Angelica told him she had never taken opera lessons and immediately suggested that she should switch to opera. But her heart remained truthful to pop music.

A few months later, while touring the country with a new show, Angelica was asked to include an opera song in her performance. Sometimes professional opera singers would go to watch the show and were intrigued to see how a pop singer could sing opera without ever taking formal opera lessons.

As her popularity grew, Angelica was chosen to perform in a show put together by a successful comedian. A year later he became her husband. Together, they played in every major city in Romania and performed many live TV shows. This tour was extended and culminated with performances in Europe, the United States, and Canada.

Her husband, already a Canadian resident for five years,

convinced Angelica that a change of domicile would be ideal. He painted a beautiful picture for Angelica of how they would be traveling together, both doing what they loved most for the rest of their lives. However, within two years, he decided instead that Angelica should give up her singing. When she found out about this decision, Angelica knew she had a difficult challenge ahead of her. Even though the pain of leaving the stage was excruciating, for the sake of her marriage she temporarily adopted the idea.

At this point her career seemed to be in the past, but deep in her heart Angelica always knew she can never deny who she really was. So she decided that she would stay focused on her inner self, her soul— the place she would later discover was the inspiration for her music.

Resourcefulness, creativity, and an enormous amount of self-discipline were Angelica's closest companions over the next few years. She found herself in a foreign country, not knowing how to speak the language and with a cloudy future ahead of her.

Nobody would hire her because she had no training in

anything other than performing on stage. For the first couple of years, she worked in telemarketing and selling gas door to door.

Things became even harder when her fifty-four year old father passed unexpectedly back home. Suddenly she felt her life was crumbling. The only escape Angelica found was in her daily vocal practice at her apartment in Toronto. However, that practice wouldn't last long. Her husband wanted her to settle down and start her life over again. He did not believe that an immigrant in her adult years would ever have a chance to make it as a singer in a foreign country, so in an attempt to save Angelica from more pain and frustration, he tried to steer her in a more "realistic" direction.

On the other hand, Angelica's mother, back in Romania, was imploring her to never give up singing: "Your father and I always knew the passion you hold. We offered you a home full of support and encouragement, but we always knew that the stage was your *real* home. Don't let anybody crush your dream now." Angelica was torn apart between her mother's words and the life change she was expected to undertake. However, her mother's words were truth and Angelica knew it. Her husband knew it also. Therefore, he became adamant that Angelica be in touch with her family as less as possible, as it was diverting her attention from the "new plan." In an attempt not to have her calls traced, she continued calling her family back home from a pay phone.

The situation was extremely challenging and because she had no one to talk to, she had no choice but to look inside herself for moral support. This proved to be the best choice because it helped her to recognize her own strength and tenacity. Angelica simply was not a quitter. She knew who she was . . . but she just didn't have the courage to say it yet. She continued training her voice, preparing to be vocally in shape for the time she *knew* she would again put it into practice. She did that, just not in anybody's presence anymore. She would wait for her husband to leave, watch his car drive out of the building's underground garage, then turn her stereo system full blast and practice. She would then keep a steady and careful watch out the window for his return.

As time passed she finally settled into the idea that more than anything, she needed to have patience and pay attention to what was around her. She began to realize it was time she took her attention off the drama in her life. She slowly gained enough strength to be open to watching the TV and seeing how others lived their dreams.

One day as she was watching a music award show, Angelica noticed something she had never seen before. The singers were performing at a level way beyond anything she thought was possible. These artists were going past their limits, reaching for perfection in ways she had never known. What she saw inspired her. She got closer to the TV and watched them for hours. There were national and international stars, pop singers, rappers, hip-hop, classical singers. She paid close attention to all aspects of their performances and recognized the key to what made them the megastars they had become: their attention to detail.

It was an eye opener for Angelica and was the first turning point for her since her arrival to Canada. She realized she had much to learn and from then on she decided that every single day would be an opportunity to become better. She started gathering knowledge; bookstores became one of her favorite places to spend time. She chose to learn about self-empowerment, the human body, make-up, hair, and nutrition, everything that would add the slightest value to the performer she knew one day she would become.

Seeking a more comfortable way to support herself, she decided to pursue training in the physical fitness profession. After completing the Fitness Leadership program at Seneca College in Toronto, she acquired her certification as a fitness assessor and consultant. What a beautiful way to keep herself in shape both physically and mentally, and what a liberating feeling to have the knowledge to not only reshape her own body in a smart, healthy way, but help others to achieve their own goals. Angelica soon became the most sought after trainer in her fitness facility.

In addition to her career, there was something else very important for Angelica to take care of: her health. The many years of living in uncertainty brought added tensions and much anxiety to her life. It was then that she knew it was time for a change. After more than five years of trying to bury her true identity inside, Angelica made the decision to free herself from her marriage, and finally felt liberated.

It took her another eight years of diligent work to regain the feeling of self-worth that her parents nourished and cherished so much in her as a child. She started writing again and the confidence she felt so naturally as a child writing in her diary, slowly returned. Her personal experiences and the freedom of finally living her life as who she really was became an unlimited pool of inspiration for her words and music. She felt the pain of leaving the stage; the joy of becoming a Canadian citizen; the moments of darkness when she was alone, tired, and discouraged; the beauty of finally being "at home" in a foreign country. And last but not least, she felt the wonder of finally finding someone who appreciates her for who she is: her new husband. His love and strong belief in Angelica's capabilities as both a singer and an author led him to put everything on the line in order to help Angelica turn her dream into reality. His selfless, uncompromising support is what enabled this CD and book to be created.

Angelica's story is not just about her growing up on stage. It's not about her passion for music and words, the commitment to her dream and the undeniable faith she discovered in herself. It's not about all the trophies and awards she has won. It's not even about the girl who once experienced fame and soon after had to give it up.

Her story is about faith, hope, willpower, and liberation. Her story is about giving everything up while holding onto the knowing that, once you are faithful to your passion, once you are faithful to who you really are, you will have that enormous strength to rise up and be that again. *Remember who you are and act upon it* is Angelica's commission to herself and also her message to you.

Please read her words and listen to her music with great care, and you will hear the voice of a spirit once again conveying the kindness, warmth, and sincerity that two parents loved so much in their little girl…

My Journey

When I first came to Canada, what caught my attention was the rich palette of wonderful opportunities this country had to offer: jobs, colleges where one could study at any age, food in abundance, heat in the winter, air conditioning in the summer, beautifully paved streets, the possibility of choosing a car and a house based on your income... There were literally hundreds of things that made me feel so blessed the moment I made this country my new home. However, along with all that, there was a very tiny question beginning to take root in my mind: "Why wasn't I born here?"

Why did I have to be born in a country where the main source of heat in the winter was the gas-cooking stove so we had to go to sleep wearing sweaters, mittens, and hats? Why did I have to be born in a country where, to provide milk for their children, mothers had to wait in line outside the grocery store at four o'clock in the morning regardless of the weather, a country where bread, oil, flour, and meat were rationed?

Why did I have to be born in a country where television programs were broadcast for only two hours a day, where it was normal to be stuck in the elevator for hours due to the government disconnecting the electricity for economic reasons, where the grocery stores carried bananas, oranges and raisins only at Christmas? Why wasn't I born here instead, and able to have the abundance Canada offered?

Why did I have to be born in a communist country and be restricted and fearful as a child, having to monitor my words very carefully because my parents could be put in jail or even go "missing" if I misspoke? Why wasn't I born here instead and able to feel the freedom of not being afraid?

Why did I have to be born in a country where for years, the songs we had sung as children were imposed upon us? Why wasn't I born in Canada and able to blossom as a singer in the way I believed I could? Instead, I found myself here as an adult, feeling fearful about the direction I wanted to take, not even knowing the language, looking to take the subway train from "Subway," the sandwich place, and feeling so silly about it later…

Without realizing it, I slowly started to resent not only where I had come from, but also where I was in the present. My determination to pursue my career in Canada was always very strong— the thought of succeeding was what actually kept me going— but at the same time I felt overwhelmed by the length of the process. It felt as if I had been born all over again, only this time already grown-up and having to bury deep inside almost everything I'd ever known, while trying to find a way to adjust to something that felt very much alien. And even though in the back of my mind *I always knew that the scenarios of both my past and my present were not the most unfortunate conditions that exist on this planet*, I was still hanging on to the question, "Why?"

Little did I know that by trying to find the answer to that question I was fighting a futile battle, keeping myself prisoner in a bubble of illusion- the illusion that I was not in charge of my own life. And by doing so, I could never find the answer to a yet deeper question, the answer that would give me the peace I was actually looking for: "Why do things happen a certain way?" Answer

I don't have all the answers, and I love the fact that I don't, simply because exploring life one step at a time is beautiful. One thing I'm sure of, however, is that my words and music are rooted in the perspective that I hold due to living my life's experiences, and that I know to be my truth. This is what my words and music are about. They are about the moment I let myself peek through my own little box and dared to be open to new possibilities. They are about the moment I felt as if a window had just opened and the freshest smell of crisp morning air touched my face and quickly filled my whole body with boundless freedom... After years of being stuck in the vicious circle of thinking that my life wasn't going anywhere it finally occurred to me: does it really matter where we are at the moment of birth? Does it really matter where we are at *any* point in our life?

Leaving the judgment behind, I finally realized how my life up until that point had nothing to do with the direction my *future* would take. The past remains the past; it cannot be changed, as hard as it may be to accept this, but what I can change is the direction my life is going. And I can do that by using one of the most valuable tools available to me at any moment in time: the freedom of choosing my own *perspective*.

The perspective we choose is what contributes to creating our moods and our emotional responses which in turn energize our experiences, carving out what we call our *destiny* with undeniable precision. I can choose to have a negative perspective and fall into the trap of feeling like a victim, kneeling with my arms raised up to the sky, asking eternally "Why?" Or I can choose to change how I am viewing the present; acknowledge the blessing of simply being born. Being born, therefore having the opportunity to feel empowered by my own desire, while holding on to the knowing that it's up to *me* to make it true.

Looking back at the conditions in my native country while holding no judgment, gives me now an incredible feeling of liberation. The conditions of life were harsh indeed, but that's all we knew. We had no model by which to compare them, since we didn't have access to the world outside our borders. So at the time, the situation didn't feel as negative as it felt when I was able to compare it with Canada, one of the best countries in the world!

Even though our leader was keeping himself occupied with creating and applying more restrictions, we still shared love with our family and friends, found reasons to laugh and enjoy each other's company; we still had beautiful bedtime stories and sang lullabies to our children. There was nothing that could make us lose sight of our inner freedom, nothing that could make us lose our hope. I remember when I was a child, there was absolutely no way anybody could pull me out of my imaginary world where every single moment was sparkling with desire and sweet anticipation of a beautiful future; my imaginary world where *anything* was possible.

Then I looked back upon the journey I had undertaken from the moment I made Canada my new home, and even though nothing is ever really wrong with anything, I wished that I hadn't let myself feel so much negative emotion. I wished that I hadn't allowed myself to be caught up in what I believed was my reality and react in ways that had actually brought upon me even more negative emotions…

Immigrating is not easy for anybody; the challenges are tangible and can be painful, especially if you are leaving a career behind, moving to a country where you don't know the language, and having to go to school in order to get a job. However, it's a process that gave me the opportunity to explore life in a much different way. It helped me realize the power in the simplicity of making a clear choice: the choice between moving along with the process or resist it; the choice between living with peace or living with pain and resentment...

I chose to feel better. I chose to look at challenges with appreciation and accept the idea that immigrating to such a beautiful country was equal to having a second chance at life. I chose to recognize the huge potential of being able to use the resources this beautiful country has to offer as an opportunity to become much stronger and much more than I had ever been before.

Changing my perspective was one of the most fulfilling and rewarding feelings I'd ever had up until that point. Looking at my past and my present through different eyes, *forgiving everything and everybody that I thought were responsible for my struggles,* helped me find the peace of mind I so needed in order to be able to look forward with courage and anticipation.

Once I let go of the weight of the judgment, my mind became clearer. And as I was learning about the power of thought, the power of intention and visualization, I realized something that stopped me in my tracks and put a smile of astonishment on my face... I remembered the very desire I had as a child, the beautiful future I kept living in my mind every single night as I was going to sleep, year after year. It was that strong, innocent desire that had paved the path for moving to a country that provided all the resources necessary to fulfill my dream. It took me thirteen years to realize that what I was resenting was my *opportunity* to fulfill my dream. It took me thirteen years to realize that what I was resenting was my *process of becoming.*

I would have never known what deep passion and true appreciation really felt like if it weren't for the times I had to give up the only thing that defined me. I've learned that music is truly my identity, and that life lived without following my passion is a life filled with unanswered questions. But mostly, I've learned that we all are pure spirit, joyful, perfect beings. Therefore, we all have the ability to get in touch with our divine Self and, while living life from that standpoint, inspire others to have the courage to reach for their own dreams.

I am not going to stay here and tell you "anything is possible," but what I am going to tell you is this: *never give up on yourself.* No matter where you are on this planet, no matter the conditions around you, it can always get better if you choose it to be better. It can always get better if you choose to adopt a positive perspective and appreciate everything that makes up your moment of *now.* It can always get better if you choose to hold on to the thought of future accomplishments instead of the thought of not wanting to be where you are. It can always get better if you focus on the clear picture of what you want to achieve and stay strong in your decision to do what makes *you* feel good. It can always get better if you stay loyal to the truth inside, if you follow your heart. Only then are limiting boundaries and man-made rules broken;

only then does "anything is possible" become more than just words, as you will feel their meaning and naturally live it.

Don't question your ability to reach heights you've never even imagined, and certainly don't let the question "How am I going to do it?" shadow your desire. The most beautiful, most rewarding part of listening to your heart is that you need not worry about *how* it will happen. You need not worry about the steps you must take toward materializing your desire. The Universe will send everything you need in order for you to accomplish what you came here to do. The right circumstances, the right people, the right words will undoubtedly make their way toward you if you trust the process and look for the beauty and the majestic purpose in everything. I know that, now…

The Story Behind the Song

Music is a powerful means of expression, and when accompanied by words that come from the place of who we really are, it can inspire and elevate. As a child I always loved writing about all that came to mind; I still do. However, writing *music* was not something I thought possible as I had never done this before. Nevertheless, I had always had a strong desire to write my own songs, so I decided to turn the stories that I had written over the years into songs.

I started by translating the essence of each story into the form of lyrics. Then something amazing happened: the lyrics dictated the melody as if the song had already existed within the story. Here I realized that when we follow our passion, the final outcome has a life and rhythm of its own. Whatever it is we are trying to accomplish, the passion behind it will give the final product its own melody. Mine just happened to come in the form of songs.

One morning I woke up, and as an unusually strong October sunray was piercing through my bedroom window, a wonderful idea came to me: I could put all my stories into book form and in this way share with you the deeper meaning of my songs. These stories are a result of the thoughts I have gathered over the years, and they represent my expression of what I believe we all are: pure, passionate and loving spirit, forever ready to unravel unlimited possibilities.

1. Feel the Feeling

Verse 1: Open the door to your heart and embrace
The warm feeling unfolding with quiet grace.
Time slows down, now be kind
To the beautiful memories floating in your mind.

Is it the memory of your child's birth
Or the memory of your first kiss?
Good memories have power, and it's worth
Holding onto their bliss.

Chorus: Feel the feeling that lies beyond words,
Feel the memory brought to you forth.
Feel the feeling, hold it in your heart,
Be the feeling and good times will come back.

Verse 2: Open the door to your heart and embrace
The wonders of life with quiet grace.
Open the door to your heart; don't be afraid to try.
Enjoy the moment gently passing by.

Is it the memory of younger days,
Feeling the freedom of play?
Look up at the stars, they can still amaze
As they did yesterday.

Chorus: Feel the feeling that lies beyond words,
Feel the memory brought to you forth.
Feel the feeling, hold it in your heart,
Be the feeling and good times will come back.

Bridge: Don't think of the past unless it brings you joy.
The present is at hand so you can shape your dreams.
The future is bright for the one who believes.

Feel the Feeling

We have no time to wait. Everything has to be effective and fast; fast transportation, fast computers, fast foods. We focus desperately sometimes on the long task lists, and we forget entirely about that part of us that is actually the only aspect of our being that would guide us toward everything that we desire. We forget about the basics of our existence, our feelings.

The feeling is not a material object that has color, texture or scent, and in our fast-paced modern society it has become the one thing that we suppress the most. We actually excel at creating "real", tangible things that can numb our feelings and artificially make us feel good for a little while. It's a vicious circle, and once caught inside, it becomes harder and harder to get out and see the bigger picture.

Frustration, disappointment, anger, depression, guilt. . . We call them "negative feelings" without realizing that once we do that, a judgment is being made. In return, the judgment creates more resistance, and consequently more negative feelings. How about stopping the judgment? How about letting your negative feelings tell you *their* story? They are the soul's way of saying that what you are focused on is not going to take you to where you want. You are headed in the wrong direction. Your negative feelings are like the rising temperature of an ill body— it's there only to let you know that something needs your attention. The fever is a *helpful* signal. That's why suppressing it is not a good idea— *finding the cause of it is.*

Go back to the basics, your feelings. Are they negative? If they are, be glad that you are aware of it. The moment you stop disregarding your negative feelings could be one of the most important points in your life because it is the moment you have the opportunity to connect to your soul and listen to what it has to say— and that is very simple: think of what *you* want for a while. Think what you want, then *feel* what you want. Give yourself the gift of quieting your mind— when you quiet your mind, the doorway to your heart will open and reveal to you the wonderful world of possibility.

...So you are quietly sitting down. You can feel the warmth of the sun coming through your window, lightly touching your face. Now, what are you going to be thinking about? What is it that you can think of, that will free you from that unpleasant feeling? Which, by the way, is an angel in disguise because it brought you the awareness of what you *do* want. So don't resent it, just take your attention away from it. Focus on the *possibility*, allow yourself to fly free within your imagination and reach for the idea of your perfect moment. Picture that perfect relationship you've always dreamed of; picture that perfect job. Break through the box and see this Universe as it actually is: a limitless creating environment. Go past the suggestion of "reality" that others impose on you and play with your imagination. It doesn't cost you anything to imagine, but the reward of doing so could soon be the gift of a life that you have always wanted.

If imagining something you've never experienced proves to be challenging, there is another way to break through and find that pleasant feeling. Go back to your past to the beautiful memories of the moments you once enjoyed. Those are the times when either knowingly or unknowingly you experienced alignment with your Inner Being— the ultimate source of clarity and power.

Be kind to those memories. Don't discard them as if they are gone forever, because they're not! Everything that we've ever lived still exists in the vibrating energy of our memories. Bring back the bliss, maybe, by remembering your younger days when freedom of play was the prevailing emotion. What comes to your mind? Is it the feeling of finally getting your favorite toy or your first bike ride? Is it the day you felt the electrifying energy of your first kiss? Or maybe the indescribable moment when time stood still as you witnessed your child's birth? Feel that feeling, and in return, it will make you feel alive again; it will empower you with the positive vibration you once experienced. You will feel stronger, much clearer in your intentions, and more open to new possibilities.

The *present* is the perfect time to decide to take a step toward making your dreams a reality. Slow down and listen to your feelings. They are there to tell you something. Change direction.

Lift your head, and with hope flickering in your eyes, firmly turn your attention toward things that put a smile on your face. And while you tenaciously hold your focus, let the winds of doubt pass you by. Greet your perfect moment with a smile. Welcome it into your life by feeling it over and over again. Let its presence unfold; let it spread its warm embrace with quiet grace. Feel its meaning go beyond what words can convey, feel the absence of need to verbalize or intellectualize it. Feel time slowing down, feel the possibility shining ahead of you and its vibrating energy coming closer and closer— feel the *inevitability* of it!

Before you know it, you will become one with it. You will *be* it! And it will make no difference if all this takes place only in your imagination, because using your imagination is the first step toward materialization— it is the spark that ignites the dream.

Don't think of your past unless it brings you joy. The present is a gift always at hand; it is the magic moment where you can shape your dreams and create your future. Think *beautiful* and the future will be brightly painted in all the colors you love.

Go back to your basics— allow yourself to feel GOOD.

2. I Am What I Am

Verse 1: A brand new day is on its way,
Ready for wonders to display.
I lift my eyes toward a sky
Revealing beauty I cannot deny.
Sometimes the clouds will come and go,
I let them be 'cause this I know:

Chorus: I am a ray of the sun
Waiting for each morning to come
So I can land somewhere.
I am what I am.
Whatever my experience here,
Could be joy and love or tears,
The sun will take me home where I belong.

Verse 2: Would you know peace is what you want
Unless you really felt discord?
Don't look around to make things right,
Rather take a look inside.
And life can turn its face to bliss
If you just remember this:

Chorus: You are a ray of the sun
Waiting for each morning to come
So you can land somewhere.
You are what you are.
Whatever your experience here,
Could be joy and love or tears,
The sun will take you home where you belong.

Bridge: Enjoy life with no fear of getting lost,
Explore yourself, do what you love most.
Doors will open and you'll see
Your answers will be clear.
Everything you've dreamed
Awaits for you to be.

Chorus: We are rays of the sun
Waiting for each morning to come
So we can land somewhere.
We are what we are.
Whatever we experience here,
Could be joy and love or tears,
Know without any doubt
That when the day turns into night,
The sun will always take us home where we belong.

I Am What I Am

A brand new day is on its way, ready to display new wonders... I lift my eyes toward the sky and I cannot help noticing its vast, never-ending beauty. I am aware that clouds may sometimes make their way toward my side of the sky and darken it for a moment or two. So I close my eyes and hold onto the picture of what's beyond the clouds— I know without doubt that they will pass. I know that the underlying beauty will shine even brighter once I've decided to remain appreciative and aware that even though I can't yet see what I wish for, it doesn't mean that it isn't there...

Undesirable times come and go just like the clouds. There are moments when we get caught up in the smaller picture and mentally lose sight of the rays that are *always* shining on the other side. We get disappointed, we feel as though we are alone, and we find it hard even to begin thinking of relying on faith...

No one enjoys feeling sad, powerless, unworthy… However, if that is where you seem to be, what do you do? How do you release yourself from those emotions? How do you sooth your troubled mind? Feeling disappointment, doubt or fear are unpleasant emotions, indeed. However, there is always a positive that comes with that. It is then that our desires begin to create our future in great depth and color because those are the moments when *we know what we really want.* How would we appreciate beauty, peace, and love if it weren't for experiencing their opposites? How would our life reveal its magnificence and beauty, if it weren't for the times when we were first gently pushed to recognize our own magnificence and beauty?

As much as we would like to be able to control the "sunshine" in our life, the truth is, at any given time, our strength lies in the ability to choose our state of mind— and that's all that we ever need to do in order to move beyond any challenge. The answer to any troubling question is only one thought away: everything is all right because there is one safe place we will always belong. No matter what, we will always be connected with the infinite intelligence— God, who never loses sight of us; it's only we who lose sight of God by falling into the trap of believing that we are powerless, limited beings...

I believe we are all coming from the same place, and we are all strong and beautiful. I believe we are free. I believe we are one with God, the Source, just as the rays of the Sun are — *forever* and *undeniably* connected. All we need is trust that there is nowhere to fall because we are who we are and that cannot be changed— ever.

So go on, explore life without fear of getting lost. Explore yourself, and do what you love most. Carry within you the knowing that this life is just a second compared to eternity and that eternity is beautiful, just as this life can be when lived with this knowing: I am a ray of the Sun, waiting joyfully for the morning to come so I can land anywhere and experience *my* choices.

. . . So I go on exploring being the light encountering a dark forest. Do I stop on the edge of it and feel powerless in front of the mystery it displays? Or hold onto the knowing that I can walk through it and spread my light and warmth everywhere it is needed?

. . . I go on filtering myself through the crystal hanging on the other side of a window and let my rays disperse in rainbow colors on someone's bedroom walls.

. . . I go on allowing myself to be transformed by the countless tiny water drops dancing in the air after the rain and know that on the other side, one of the most beautiful phenomena will appear— a rainbow— which may put a smile on the face of the one looking up to the sky for answers.

I am a ray of the Sun… So wherever I go and whatever I experience— whether it's love or joy, whether it be tears or pain— I can never be lost in it because *I am what I am*, and ultimately and without any doubt, when the night comes, the Sun will always bring me back home where I belong.

3. Strong

Verse 1: Controlling thoughts, controlling words
Have tried to shut my song.
I didn't look beyond the darkness,
Thinking that I was wrong.

Verse 2: He cut my wings
And tried to give me a destiny,
And told me with a smiling face
That's where I wanted to be.

Chorus: Controlling thoughts, controlling words
Have tried to shut my song.
One day I looked inside my heart
And found something I knew all along: I'm strong.

Bridge: Strong enough to let my truth shine,
I'm strong enough to genuinely smile.
I'll open my arms and find love again,
I'm strong enough to show and say who I am.

Chorus: Controlling thoughts, controlling words
Have tried to shut my song.
One day I looked inside my heart
And found something I knew all along: I am strong.

$\mathcal{S}$trong

There was a time in my life when I believed that things were happening for a reason; that I was destined to meet certain people and go through very specific emotions. It seemed everything was beyond my control and as time passed I began to shut down my feelings and convinced myself that it was all happening for some mysterious reason… A reason I would never find the answer simply because it was not meant to be found. So I was living each day humbly accepting what was unfolding for me, while suffering inside tremendously…

I put my trust and dreams in the hands of someone who I thought wished only the best for me. And he probably did; only his "best for me" did not match *my* version… I unknowingly gave away the power of being in charge of my own life, which in turn made me so vulnerable to the point where I was no longer deciding anything I was about from the moment

I awoke until I fell asleep at night; I was no longer deciding my own future.

The moment I accepted the pretense of being someone else (which was the moment I did not voice my questions and my truth), I felt as though I was endlessly falling. Despite feeling that way, I did what I was told and allowed myself to be uprooted from the life I'd been building since I was a child— I stopped doing what gave me peace. The illusion built around me was so strong that I never questioned anything. I simply took the circumstances as they were, and in order to find some relief, I almost convinced myself that it would be wrong and selfish of me to continue being who I am. Even though my feelings were constantly signaling me to reconsider the choices I was making, I kept disregarding them.

~ I didn't know that I shouldn't allow anyone to structure my destiny or let myself be blinded by a smiling face telling me that his vision was the life I wanted but I just didn't realize it yet…

~ I didn't know that sometimes people put limitations on their loved ones in order to hide their own weaknesses…

~ I didn't know that by not taking charge of my own life I was hurting not only myself but also the people who loved me most dearly, my parents and siblings…

~ I didn't know that by allowing my gift of free choice to be taken away I was creating a bigger and bigger gap between myself and God.

When we do something because someone else wants us to and we feel negative emotions, we are not being true to who we really are— we move away from our center. We can never actually break the connection we have with our divine Selves, but we can stray quite far from it and as a result endure the strong emotions that follow. In doing this, not only are we not doing a favor to ourselves but we are not helping the other person as well— he or she will never learn one of the most valuable lessons in life: to find their happiness within themselves not in trying to change the other.

When somebody affects anyone in a negative way, when they act from fear rather than Love and understanding, they don't feel the benefit of giving, and therefore experiencing security and peace. Also by *being allowed* to interfere in someone else's experience, they never learn. And so they keep hiding behind this mask they've adopted along life's trail, a mask that becomes harder and harder to bear. Their negative outbursts are actually a scream for help … Living in this continuous struggle, having lost sight of their divine nature, *they* are the ones who feel powerless; *they* are the ones who truly need help.

When I found myself with my back against the wall and had nowhere else to go, when I was forced to unwillingly take a break from punishing myself by allowing someone else to do so, when machines were hooked up to my heart showing me what I had done to it, that's when I recognized I had come to a fork in the road. I *had* to make a choice.

Supported by faith and hope, my mind searched further

for an answer. And there it was. . . waiting patiently within my heart shining in all its glory: it was absolutely no one's fault that I was where I was. No one's. *I* had asked for it— very clearly. I had asked for it every single time I believed myself to be a victim, every single time I thought I was not appreciated. I asked for it every time I believed that there was no perfect relationship and that I had to constantly be on my toes working at the one I had. I asked for it every single time I didn't think of myself as a person worthy of finding someone to accept me as I am, believing the delusion that something like that didn't exist...

However, my true Self knows... It knows I am worthy and if I just turn my attention inward and listen, truth will always be a statement to prove it. And it did this by putting in front of me *exactly* what I had asked for: somebody who was a mirror image of my own thoughts, a person who with great clarity reflected back to me my own beliefs and fears— a person who actually came to teach me my own strength.

All those thoughts flashed through my mind awakening me to my own life— I finally let my heart decide.

I suddenly felt safe and free. Listening to my heart opened the door to the unlimited potential that true love always has to offer. I grew up believing that true love is only found in another but listening to my heart showed me that true love is actually the essence of who we all are, it is the essence of who I am. Therefore I am strong beyond my imagination; strong enough to genuinely smile; strong enough to let the feeling of worthiness light up my face; strong enough to open my arms and let "the one" find his way into my experience.

I understood that any time people use anything less than love as a means to express themselves, is because they have temporarily forgotten who they are. Then I understood that there is something much better for me to choose to feel in those moments other than hurt and disappointment. I can simply choose to be true to myself and in this way maybe inspire others realize they are much more than what they believe...

Each new day I find what an incredible feeling of liberation it is to gently, yet firmly let my truth shine and live as who I really am— always.

"Selfishness is not living as one wishes to live;
it is asking others to live as one wishes to live."
~ Oscar Wilde ~

4. Love Gives You the Freedom

Verse 1: I look at the world
Divided by lines of illusion,
I look at the people
Running on empty, going in circles,
Trying to find the answer.

Chorus: Love gives you the freedom you are looking for,
Love gives you the freedom, it opens all doors.
Nothing else in this life can give you true peace.
Give love with all your heart
And learn about forgiveness.

Verse 2: Birds need wings to fly
The sun rising needs a sky
The trees need wind to whisper
The lost one needs to wander

The ocean needs a shore to embrace and kiss
People need love to enjoy all this...

Chorus: Love gives you the freedom you are looking for,
Love gives you the freedom, it opens all doors.
Nothing else in this life can give you true peacc.
Give love with all your heart
And learn about forgiveness.

Bridge: Each of us desires so many different things
But deep inside there is one song that we all sing.
Let it shine; let it rise like a flower from a seed.
Love is kind, it never fails, it's all we need.

Chorus: Love gives you the freedom you are looking for,
Love gives you the freedom, it opens all doors.
Nothing else in this life can give you true peace.
Give love with all your heart
And learn about forgiveness.

Love Gives You the Freedom

Sitting peacefully on my veranda, I'm watching the flow of movement on my street: cars passing by, people going in and out of their homes, children rollerblading or riding bikes. I can feel the energy of the subtle sounds coming from all directions, unifying and rising up into one soft body filled with vibrating, precious life. I can't help but notice that while I can see that everybody is enjoying the beauty of this day, the underlying driving force of this life movement is that every single person is in fact searching for something. No matter how significant or insignificant it may seem, we are all searching for something.

As simple as this observation may seem to be, I realize that it's actually not. We are all looking for something. You might say, "Okay, and . . . ?" Well, what lies beyond every single want? A desire to feel good. You might say, "Okay, I know that! I want something because I know it will make me feel better." Then I say, "Then why is it that shortly after we get what we want, our appreciation of it fades?" You might say, "It's because we are eternally evolving and, therefore, wanting something that can serve our continual, constant evolution." And I say, "That's very good, but what is your state of mind *before* you get your next toy? Are you happy? Are you living with passion and positive expectation in *between* your wants?"

So far, I haven't met too many people who can honestly say they are truly happy, but I'm sure there are many. What I'm talking about here definitely does not apply to everybody, and it surely doesn't apply to children, but it does apply to me, and many people I know.

So we want something, and then we get it, but shortly thereafter we lose the bliss. Then we want something else, we get it, and lose the bliss. What is it that we are actually looking for?

We all desire so many different things, based on the different conditions under which we each live, but the truth is that deep inside we are all looking for exactly the same thing. In essence our souls sing the exact same tune…

The root of every desire we have is to feel connected. We are looking for the ultimate source of well-being, the one that's always there; ready to give us the most satisfying feeling— the feeling of completeness, the feeling of freedom. Birds need wings to fly, the sun needs a sky in which to rise and set, trees need the wind to whisper, and a question needs an answer. The ocean needs a shore to embrace with each wave; the lost one needs to wander before finding himself. Everything finds its resolution in one steady thing. People need love to feel truly alive and enjoy all the wonders of life. From there, everything else becomes easy, and our life purpose can unfold as clearly as a well-written book.

Love is kind. Love never fails. Love is all we need. In giving love, we get in return the freedom we hope to find through the fulfillment of our desires. Fulfilling our desires gives a feeling of freedom indeed, yet the best way to accomplish anything long lasting and real is through love. It's a full circle. Giving love opens the doors to an unlimited horizon, filled with every imaginable accomplishment ready for us to choose; it connects us with our true Self, it gives us clarity and inspiration.

There is nothing in all life that can give us more peace than opening our hearts to the truth of who we really are—beings who are able to look upon everybody and everything through the eyes of true forgiveness: knowing in reality that *there is nothing to forgive.*

Once you truly feel that, then deep appreciation will come naturally. When your teenage child rebels, you will not forget the incredible feeling you had when he or she was born. You will never again put yourself down for not accomplishing all your tasks in one day, but instead you will appreciate that you are doing your very best. You will never allow unpaid bills to frustrate you to the point where you fall out of love with your spouse— the one you fell in love madly the day you met.

You will find joy not only in your newly acquired valuables but also in the ones that you were so ready to replace. Not to say that we shouldn't discard anything— because we are evolving beings, technology is moving rapidly forward, and we are expanding endlessly— but it's one thing to want a bigger house while resenting the house you're in, and it's a totally different thing to want a bigger house while appreciating the roof that has kept you covered when you needed it. The fastest way to get to what we want is to choose to reevaluate our perception of *now*. Appreciating the moment of now is the shortcut to the fulfillment of our desires.

We want to feel good because we innately know that feeling good gives us a true sense of security, which is what being connected really is about. We ultimately want to have love as the foundation of our actions and to feel the comforting vibration of the freedom it gives. Love gives us the freedom we are searching for. Freedom, in turn, gives us the means to be peaceful and creative. Love gives us freedom, which connects us to our soul. Love gives us freedom, which is one way of defining the soul.

5. You're My Reflection

Verse 1: Drops of rain are falling on the ground,
And they're slowly taking your shape and sound.
Every time I look around, every time I smile,
Your beauty is what I see smiling back at me.

Chorus: You're my reflection,
My soul's expression.
My love for you goes far beyond the sun,
I know that you and I are one.

Verse 2: Every time you smile out to the world,
It feels as if divine Love is right here, in my hand.
I wish I could share this power with all wandering souls,
So they too feel as surreal as how you make me feel.

Chorus: You're my reflection,
My soul's expression.
My love for you goes far beyond the sun,
I know that you and I are one.

Bridge: So many years of wandering
And searching for someone,
In your arms now, I'm home.

Chorus: You're my reflection,
My soul's expression.
My love for you goes far beyond the sun,
I know that you and I are one.

You're My Reflection

Every night as I was falling asleep, I knew in my heart that somebody like you existed in my time-space reality, and that very soon I would feel the divine connection that I had only read about in Cinderella stories. I was feeling in love, in love with someone I hadn't even met yet. My friends thought I was crazy, but I knew what I was feeling. I could feel the gentle wave preceding something wonderful that was about to happen…

I was walking down the street, enjoying a gentle refreshing rain blessing everything it touched on its way to the ground. As I watched the drops of water fall from the sky, a feeling came to me that the rain is one of nature's ways of reminding us to let go of the past, and wait for a new beginning with positive expectation... The raindrops were gathering in puddles on the pavement, slowly taking the form and sound of you, "the one" I was yet to find: I could clearly see the gentle features of your beautiful face, I could feel the joy in your smile, I could hear the sound of your sweet voice calling me to you. Was it the rain revealing your presence to me? Or was I creating you with my desire, using the rain as my brush and the pavement as my canvas? You are now part of my life, and I can clearly see why…

You showed me myself. You stood in front of me and just like a mirror showed me myself. You knew exactly who I was without me ever saying a word, and you helped me to see it too. With no desire to correct anything, you were so innocently amazed at my perfection— perfection I never believed until you gave me this irrefutable explanation: I am a child of that which is perfect; I am a child of God, so how can I not be perfect? What a beautiful, most precious gift! To help someone recognize that he or she is perfect, and as a result, something even more wonderful takes place: that someone perceives everyone else in the same way. *I love you for gently guiding me to find my own unlimited potential and beauty.*

You are so innocent. I look into your eyes and can't help but smile, knowing that your eyes will never age, simply because you look upon everything through the eyes of an ever-innocent child. It's a privilege to watch you interact so gracefully with the people around you, always giving them your straightforward loving thought, never allowing your actions to be altered by the shadows of pretense. I look at you and I feel so very special to have in my life such a beautiful person I can call my own. *I love you for not being afraid to show your innocence even when you know some people mistake it for naivety.*

You are my reflection. Whatever I say I want to accomplish you believe is possible. Your answers to my dreams are like an echo of my own thoughts. Hindering me or anything that encompasses my persona is not part of your agenda; supporting everything that I am is. Even in the midst of turmoil, you taught me how to live through anything by holding onto the power of divine love and, with its breath right here in the palm of my hand, draw my inspiration from its unlimited resources. It makes me want to share this feeling with all those souls who believe they are lost, so that they may feel just as loved and empowered, and just as beautifully surreal. *I love you for showing me that when one holds onto love, giving up hope becomes impossible.*

You are my soul's expression. I wouldn't be surprised if one day I discovered that each soul expresses the qualities of "the one." I wouldn't be surprised if one day I learned that the soul comes to earth already knowing that "the one" he or she sculpted through divine expression exists already, and is here within one's reach. I wouldn't be surprised if one day I found out that my soul painted the picture of you, as a desire to be with and have a life filled with the joy of being together as one. I love you for allowing me to be part of your life in a way I've never even dreamed— the most secure, trust-based way. When I am in your arms, you truly make me feel the power and the serenity of being at home.

My love for you goes far beyond what the eye can see and the mind can perceive. Using words can be a very powerful way to express what we feel, but the soul's language has no words and therefore no barriers. Its language is freedom. So I let my soul connect with yours, and together feel the divine unity that needs no words to be described.

"The reason I love you
is something you can't see in the mirror."
~ Dr. Kenneth G. Mills ~

6. The Sun Sent Me a Ray (to keep forever)

Verse 1: In the stillness of the night,
In the greatness of the sun
I felt your soul wandering around,
That's when it all began.

Chorus: And now that you're here
It feels like the sun sent me a ray to keep forever.
Beautiful ray of divine light
Can turn into gold even the darkest night.
Beautiful ray reminding me
To look for the beauty in everything I see.

Verse 2: You teach to embrace each day
With pure innocence and truth.
Little steps show me the way
To eternal youth.

Chorus: And now that you're here
It feels like the sun sent me a ray to keep forever.
Beautiful ray of divine light
Can turn into gold even the darkest night.
Beautiful ray reminding me
To look for the beauty in everything I see.

The Sun Sent Me a Ray (to keep forever)

The day before you were born, you came into my dream exactly the way you are: strikingly beautiful, with a strong mind, ready to operate innately by listening to your feelings, making no compromises when it came to your truth— which, by the way, is the meaning of your name!

Then the day came, and you decided it was time to open your eyes to the wonders of the world you chose. You looked right into my eyes with this unusual mature curiosity, and I knew in that moment that my life turned around and attached to itself a deeper meaning than I could ever possibly imagine…

I looked at you, and seeing you so small and gentle I suddenly felt overwhelmed by the thought that I needed to protect you from something. I wished that before you even took your first step, I could instill in you, in one breath alone, all the wisdom and knowledge I had been blessed to learn, and maybe save you from the same struggle and hard lessons. Yes, the physical world can sometimes be overwhelming (due to our beliefs, of course, but that's another story), but if we fall for it, we miss precious moments of life and one of the reasons we came here: to birth dreams and find a way to embrace the journey of turning them into reality; find a way to appreciate everything you feel, everything you do, everything you are and everything you are not. Staying connected to your true Self will give you the empowering understanding that everything you desire is on its way to you; it will help you appreciate not always having the answer, while *knowing* that you have the power to find it.

Life is about experiencing. It is what we experience that makes us desire new things, and as hard as it may be to accept, it seems that it is mostly our negative experiences, or so we call them, that help us be more clear about what we really want. The very thought that one day you might experience pain made me feel weak inside, sucked in by the awful feeling that negative thoughts can give. I didn't want to think that one day you might experience something that would bring tears to your eyes. But then again, how would you ever be able to choose if I were to cry your tears?

I pushed all thoughts of fear and insecurity away, and I

chose to have another look at you instead— so peaceful and beautiful, so fresh and hopeful, but mostly so deceivingly weak! I suddenly realized you already had the knowing built within you. You were using the life-giving breath perfectly, you cried when you were hungry and when you needed my touch; you smiled when I held you and felt soothed when I talked to you; you always trusted that I was there, ready to comfort and wrap you up in my endless, warmest love. You had no words in your vocabulary, yet you never failed to let me know exactly what you needed in every single moment. Your "just be" type of existence created this mutual, easy-to-understand dialog between the two of us and showed me that the intentions and the feelings we hold are much stronger than all the words in the dictionary put together.

I also realized that if I am in charge of anything it would be to *allow* you to experience what you came here to experience. I know I am not here to tell you what to do or not to do, but gently guide you to always look for the answers you are seeking within your heart. I can show you how knowing who I am serves me, and allow you to choose whether or not to follow my example. I can show you that whichever path you take is perfectly fine because it is *your* life and you are in charge of it— nobody else. I am to quietly watch your steps, while allowing you to move freely on your path to eternal innocence and youth. I am to appreciate and nurture your "anything is possible" state of being, and relax into the knowing that your attitude of total ease will only draw to you the best things in life.

I looked at you and realized that you are my teacher and that I am to nourish your purity and clarity of thought and take example from it. I looked at you and realized the fresh flicker in your eyes was telling me quietly about the beautiful, infinite possibilities of this life, reminding me that I too came into this world knowing no limits, but somewhere along the way I lost sight of it…

I looked at you and realized that besides all the sleepless nights and all the feelings of frustration from doubting that I was a perfect mom, you were telling me in each and every moment, "Don't worry mommy, you're doing just fine!"

I looked at you and realized that I was blessed beyond

imagination to have such a fresh being in my arms, a being that had just come from a place of total certainty and freedom, beaming out a strong message that life shouldn't be as complicated as I make it out to be.

From the moment you came into my life I feel as if the sun has sent me a ray to keep forever— a beautiful, divine ray showing me the way, quietly reminding me to look only for the beauty in everything; a light-giving ray, shining strong and clear, warming my heart like nothing ever has before, teaching me how to release doubt and trust in the beautiful nature that I am. A pure ray, innocently showing me how the simplicity of believing can give one the power to turn the darkest forest into gold and climb the highest mountain with ease and appreciation.

I cherish and adore you. I have the utmost respect for who you are. And if even for a second I forget any of these words, please remind me of your divine perfection, and also of mine. Because some time ago, somewhere far away, another young woman felt as though the sun had sent her a ray to keep forever, in the moment *I* decided to come into this world…

7. Givers of Light

Verse 1: We're trying so hard to find that something
That puts our life at ease.
We're praying that God would give us
The answer to His quiz.

We're trying to bring some light
In our own innocent way,
But if the light's not bright enough,
We judge ourselves at the end of each day.

Chorus: Nobody's wrong and nobody's right,
It's just the way things are.
We just forget once in a while
To look up at our own star.

Let's try to understand
Love without conditions.
Nobody's wrong and nobody's right,
We're all givers of light.

Verse 2: I know you're tired; just stop a moment—
The answer is in your heart.
You just be true to yourself,
And live your life as who you really are.

We need not to pretend,
We need no made-up vows;
The only vow we ever need
We make with love within our own hearts.

Givers of Light

We all come from the same place. We all have sparkles in our eyes, good things to say, love to give, but often we are troubled by busy schedules and by the rules and limitations we put upon ourselves. Some of us even think that life is some sort of a school where, once enrolled, we have no choice but to go through all these challenging tests, and if we don't find the right answers, we fail.

In reality, every single one of us is moving gracefully through life, doing the best that we can. The motivation behind everything we do is the desire to bring some light into our lives and our loved ones' lives. Our intentions are noble, but then we allow the feeling of unworthiness to take over, and then what do we do when the lights are turned out at the end of each day? We assess, we judge what *didn't* work out, what we *didn't* accomplish that day, and focus our attention on what *could have been better*. Then we get tired of our own thoughts and finally decide to go to sleep, hoping (unrealistically) to have a peaceful rest.

Then next morning we wake up looking for the sun. If rain clouds cover the blue sky, we have already figured out how to start our conversation with the stranger in front of us at the coffee shop: "Miserable day, huh?" Then we go on rushing through our day and in one way or another, putting ourselves into some sort of competition: competition with others or ourselves…

Competition with oneself can be deceiving. Do you compete with the "you" from yesterday, trying even harder to accomplish your tasks, hoping to please others? Or do you only want to excel at what you do because it makes *you* feel good inside?

Competition with others can be deceiving too. When you look up at the sky at night, what thoughts do you hold? Are you feeling appreciation for all the flickering stars lighting up the sky? Or do you focus your gaze upon your star and worry that it's not shining as brightly as others? Some stars are just closer, you know; they only *seem* to shine more brightly…

And yes, others might be doing better, but did you ever stop and wonder why they are doing better? Maybe it is because they choose to use their valuable energy on ways to improve their lives, accomplish their desires, and do something they are passionate about. Maybe it is because they live their lives without bringing anyone else's success into the equation as a basis of comparison. Maybe their basis of comparison is how they feel with regard to anything they are doing. Maybe they are doing better because they are not looking outside themselves to find the definition of success.

Sometimes we have a habit of entertaining the right-and-wrong game. Being a winner implies that there is a loser. Being right implies that somebody else is wrong. In reality, everyone has a different perspective from which they look at things, and things look differently depending on where you are standing. Everyone experiences a different upbringing, different school systems, different parents, different countries, or different governments. That's how our beliefs are being born, and that's where our perspective and actions arise from. I'm not trying to say that it is okay for people to hurt each other. My only point is that unreleased grief, hatred, intolerance, and lack of forgiveness only weigh one down and don't resolve the problems in any way.

      We know by now that whatever we give attention to is what we attract. So, by putting our attention on something we consider not right, we attract more of those "not right" situations. Then we wonder why we find more and more people doing the things we don't agree with: "What's gotten into this world?" Nothing has gotten into this world. Everything around us is exactly the way it's supposed to be— it is the result of what we attract through our thoughts, beliefs, and expectations.

      Being in a judgment mode weighs us down. Trying to be right no matter what doesn't lead us anywhere but to a lonely existence. Dropping the judgment is like embarking on a hot-air balloon ride— you go up high in the sky and are able to see the world from the place where the light of the sun prevails, the place where "perspective" looses all meaning. Everything is at our fingertips for us to change if we only decide to do so. If we only turn our attention toward our desired goals, the world…well, it might not change, but our *perception* of it will. And don't be surprised if one day, while you are wrapped up in the comforting feeling of appreciation, the colors of the world begin to brighten before your very eyes…

Be happy knowing that you shine as brightly as any star. You are just as capable of achieving anything you want as the most successful person you know. There is no real difference between you and him or her— there is only the difference that you *believe* there is.

We think that God has created life as a mystery quiz for us and that we are most likely destined to fail∴ And what is it exactly that we can fail? The answer is "nothing". There are no schools, no quizzes, no tests, no marking of our answers; there are no winners or losers. Nobody is wrong and nobody is right— we are all givers of light.

Not allowing the truth of who we are to come forth is like pretending to be someone we are not. We don't need to pretend we are anything. We don't need to try to find the most beautiful vows to tell each other. Whether words are spoken or not, we can feel their power through the clear intention coming forth from within: I am everyone and everyone is I. I am a child of the Light which shines in me and in everyone. I am going to live and allow others to be as they are; because it's only through allowing that I will know mySelf. Whether it's through a word, a gesture, a thought or just a smile, I will allow.

"An eye for an eye makes the whole world blind."
- Mahatma Gandhi -

8. Your Love

Verse 1: Your love is perfect in my eyes.
It's easy to describe to you why
It gives inspiration and meaning
To the way I'm feeling.

Your love is sitting in my heart
Wrapping me up from inside out.
It gives me strength and never lets me fall,
The best feeling of all.

Chorus: The most complete, assuring love
Love that knows no doubt or fear.
Now I know where I come from,
Now I know I was never alone.

Verse 2: I love our never-ending dance,
Music of the soul set a perfect pace.
Your magic pirouettes spread love across
With no sense of loss.

Chorus: The most complete, assuring love
Love that knows no doubt or fear.
Now I know where I come from,
Now I know I was never alone.

Bridge: I know the real feeling is lying beyond words
That's the place my wounds are healing.
Your love is lifting me up heavenwards,
Carrying me to a bright beginning.

Now I know where I come from
Now I know I was never alone,
I can never be alone.

Your Love

Your Love is what gives the word "perfection" its meaning. Your Love flows like a river of never-ending inspiration, and when we trust it and let ourselves be taken away by it, we understand the meaning of our life; we feel the deep connection to our own being— we truly know where we came from and who we really are.

Your Love is the most assuring and complete Love; it knows no doubt or fear. Your Love is kind, understanding and patient, and is always there as a permanent reminder that we can *never* be alone.

Your Love is gentle, yet strong— so strong that not only can it turn us around and make us feel worthy in our own eyes, but it can turn whole worlds around as there is nothing that is too big or too powerful that can stand in its way. Your Love is that which I translate to mean God, the Creator, the Source, Divine, Inner Being, or whatever words one chooses to define The Absolute.

Your Love is the eternal, unconditional Love and the place from which we all emerge. We are eternal beings, being naturally in love— that is our foundation. Children inherit characteristics and physical features from their parents. Let's look at the big picture and when we recognize each one as a child of God, we will come to the realization that it would be impossible for us to have been born without any trace of Love— it is the essence of who we are. The question is, do we listen to Its call or do we deny it? Do we allow ourselves to operate from that natural magnificent impulse, or do we simply suppress it?

We all know the feeling of being aligned with Love. It is the feeling that comes forth from within in many moments of our lives. It is what we felt when we were just born, it is what we continued to feel in our early years, but then it gradually faded as we allowed the drama of daily life to take over. We still feel it once in a while, but often we don't recognize it as the light from within beaming out the strong message of who we truly are.

We feel it when we are in love; we feel it when we hold our children tightly; we feel it as the tears stream down our cheeks while watching a beautiful romance on the screen; we feel it when we immerse ourselves in what we love doing most to the point where we lose track of all time. These are all moments when we naturally allow God's love to shine through from deep inside— the moments of aligning with who we are.

How about *deliberately* letting this Love to wrap you up from the inside out? How about allowing this Love to fully define you, letting It show what it can do for you…? In the magnificent moment when you surrender to It, all your questions will be answered and all your doubts cleared. You will find yourself in this never-ending dance where the soul set the perfect music with a perfect pace. Allow it to lead and you will soon be twirling in magical pirouettes, abundantly spreading Love around without feeling any sense of loss… You will understand that giving is receiving. You will recognize the magic that is *you* and what you call "miracles" will be within your reach to claim and experience. The impossible becomes possible. It's through this Love that you can bypass the physicality, consciously connect with your ever-awakened spirit, and find peaceful resolution to any challenge by drawing inspiration from Its loving ways.

This Love gives you the security of knowing that you can never fall and, better yet, the knowing that there is nowhere to fall. Let your eyes see beyond the boundaries of reality, and a different picture will unfold before you: anywhere you'll look— above, below, to your right or left, straight ahead or behind you— you'll find these infinite rays of light holding you tightly, yet giving you the ultimate freedom; wrapping themselves around you, going through you, and then stretching out to the point where they become the horizon. Your body starts humming, overflowing with warm, positive vibrations as each and every cell is being filled with majestic light waking you up to your life's purpose…

And if we all did that, we each would finally feel the power of Oneness— our universes interconnecting with each other, expanding into a perfect light-giving sphere, so powerful that with just one gentle breath it could take down all the walls of illusion we've been building between us for thousands of years. . .

Words, however, can only take the meaning of God's Love so far… Only to the point where feeling without the need of words begins. It is there that Love will lift you heavenwards, gently carrying you toward a place of bright beginnings; a new, yet familiar place where your wounds are healed and your overwhelmed mind is restored, a place of utter awe and appreciation of All that Is— the place where Freedom lives.

9. Remember Who You Are

Verse 1: You're facing now the end of a road
Paved with illusions and what others want.
You know it's not supposed to be this way,
There're feelings inside and words you can't say.

And you try and hope to break through your sadness
Holding onto beliefs of what life should be like.
Nothing else left to say but to cherish your greatness.
Answers are easy for the pure of heart to find.

Chorus: Remember who you are,
Release your inner child.
Remember who you are,
Quiet your mind, let your soul guide.

Verse 2: Losing yourself in games and fake smiles,
It only shows you who you are not.
It's all right if you lost your way for a while.
It's time to be still, the truth lies inside.

Nothing else left to say but to cherish your greatness.
Answers are easy for the pure of heart to find.

Chorus: Remember who you are,
Release your inner child.
Remember who you are,
Quiet your mind, let your soul guide.

Bridge: Wherever you are, whatever you do,
Remember and know that love is in you.

Remember Who You Are

When a baby decides to open her eyes to the wonders of this world, her parents tend to lovingly assume that they are in charge of paving the way for her; sometimes they spend too much time worrying about what their baby is going to do or be... She will pave her own way, as nobody can *see* more clearly than she does. It is through her own desires and decisions that her life will take shape and meaning. It is through her own choices that her wonderful physical existence will come to the fulfillment of its purpose.

The child lives her first years of life based on the natural life impulse from which she was born, moving freely in her own limitless universe. Unfortunately it's not too long before she finds herself being stopped in her tracks by the worry-based actions displayed by either parents, relatives, or teachers— basically those who are in charge of the child's upbringing, education, and, ultimately, her future. They don't do that because they have bad intentions. They only do that because they were taught the same way by their parents and teachers and are simply passing on the ideas they have adopted themselves.

Each and every one of us came from a place of knowing who we are, a place where everything is looked upon through the eyes of love— the perspective of boundlessness and limitlessness. Young children still have that fresh in their minds, which is why "You can't do that!" feels as if their power is being taken away— it feels unnatural. A child's natural impulse is to explore everything that surrounds them. It's how they get to know their world and become accustomed to it. We parents would be of so much more assistance and help if we allowed our children to find their own answers— within the parameters of safety, of course— however, many times the predominant word used by some parents with their children is "No" even when the situation is perfectly safe…

It's become a common belief that children are to be looked upon as beings that have no experience when it comes to life. In a way that is true. At the same time, children have what most adults have forgotten: the clarity to listen to their inner voice, the courage to act based on how they feel, and the eagerness to explore. Once a parent decides to nourish that, the child will create a life filled with unique, positive, and fulfilling experiences.

Children don't need us to give them examples of what went wrong in our experience! All they need is encouragement that they are on the right track if they are listening to their own heart and intuition. Have faith in them instead of worrying and this will encourage them to make decisions that will serve their own unique expansion. As adults, we must remember that it's not the age of a body that defines one's wisdom, but one's capacity to remember who one is. Children do so naturally— they know who they are much more than we think we know who they are...

As with everything in life, repetition is what creates a strong, solid foundation; repetition is what creates habit. What happens when someone else's beliefs are constantly enacted before you, especially at a very young age? What happens when you hear the same thing over and over again? You start adopting them as your own beliefs, and they become the foundation of your actions.

So, you grow up learning that life is mostly about following rules and directions and trying to fit in. Sometimes you play games without even knowing: you smile when you don't feel like it just to please your boss, your spouse, or anybody you believe something in your life depends upon. You do favors while feeling tired, depressed, or frustrated without realizing that you are not doing any good to anybody that way. The result is living day to day feeling trapped in the belief that you are not in charge of your own life.

While walking down this road paved with illusions and other people's expectations of what you should do or be, you sense something is off. You feel the conflicting waves of energy in your body; your mind speaks words you can't really verbalize. You try to break through these overwhelming sensations, while unknowingly holding onto old beliefs that keep you where you are… You want to break free, but others are telling you that it's just not possible, you've got responsibilities now, you shouldn't worry, it's normal— all grown-ups go through this, just get some anti-depressants and keep going!

When the night comes, you sit down and watch actors on the screen who are breaking boundaries and turning their dreams into reality. You have a dream too, but you quickly dismiss it: anything is possible in a film. Still, you *know* you have a dream, and if somebody were to ask you, "What would you choose to be or do if you knew you could not fail?" you would have an immediate answer. And while speaking about it, your eyes would light up, and your voice would sound like a rhythmically flowing song. In those powerful moments of clarity you break through the overwhelming sensation of limits and effortlessly reach for the child in you, the child who is a reminder of the sweet freedom you once tasted with your whole being— you are talking about your *dream*!

And what is a "dream" anyway? It is something we believe to be out of the ordinary, almost impossible to achieve, something that only exists in one's imagination. And when someone does achieve it, we say it was fate, luck, or a miracle. That's why we call it a "dream".

Some have become very good at covering up the

resentment which comes from not having the courage to reach for their dreams. They deny their feelings and trick themselves into superficially feeling "better", all the while having underlying emotions of regret. Others hope to live their dreams through their children. As a result, they tend to push them to chase what they didn't have the courage to do, and in this way fail greatly at noticing their children's own innate capabilities and precious talents— the root of their own passion.

However, you can break free from that vicious circle of playing hide-and-seek with your life's purpose. Drop the judgment and rekindle your innocence. Allow your inner child to be released; let it playfully guide you back into remembering. You might ask, "Remember what?" *Remember who you are.* Remembering who you are will give you the most satisfying, blissful experience there is, because it will reveal to you your true identity, your purpose.

Be kind to yourself and take time to sit quietly. Listen to the rhythm of your breath. Listen to the beating of your heart. Listen to your feelings. Listen to what's inside and you'll hear a

voice that will never deceive you. Allow it to have the last word…
No matter how old, talentless, insignificant, or inappropriate you
think you are, what's inside you is much stronger than the image
you have of yourself. What's inside you will always see you as the
most elegant, most beautiful, perfect human being, simply because
you are.

You will then realize that what you call a "dream" is not
unattainable, because you are that— *you are your dream*. You
dream of it because from deep within your soul is showing you the
way to feeling your completeness and your worth.

Are you looking to find peace and tranquility? Are you
looking for purpose? Try to remember who you are. Allow your
mind to accept it, embrace it, feel it, and cherish it as your ultimate
truth.

"Love resides within,
patiently waiting to express itself through your passion."
- *Angelica* -

10. Canto Della Terra

You might me wondering why have a Classical song in a Pop album... As unusual as this may seem, for me it's the next logical step— I finally remembered who I am. To be exact, I finally *accepted* who I am. For many years I have been thinking and writing about the great importance of remembering who we are, but never did it occur to me to assess myself. I thought I had that part all figured out. I recently realized I didn't.

I've been pushing away this side of me, not recognizing the actual love I have for classical music. I always thought of it as being one separate aspect; something that just "happened" to come naturally. For years I didn't take it seriously and never listened to people advising me to pursue it. And even worse, I never listened to my inner voice.

I finally accepted my being as a whole. Looking back, it's very clear that I knew it all along. So what happened then, considering I'm so adamant about finding my true identity? How did I let this happen to me?

This proved to me, once again, that paying attention to "what's out there" rather than what's in(side), along with a lack of trust in oneself, are some of the things that can greatly influence one's choices.

I finally made a choice to stop pushing against what came naturally. Since I had never received classical training, I decided to take voice lessons from an experienced voice coach before I recorded a classical song. A couple of months later, I recorded "Canto Della Terra".

You might ask "So what's next, Pop or Classical?" I will continue training and treat my voice as one. I love singing and writing music, and will continue to do so. I am thrilled and very excited about the idea of recording my next album. As to the direction I am going to take, I will tell you this: it will be *me*.

Epilogue

"Life is a roller coaster," some of us say. And just like one, set in concrete and steel, life will unfold unexpected up's and down's. It's almost a habit when something good happens to immediately think that the opposite will follow. We put ourselves in a state of *expectation*, which is a very powerful state— when we expect, we project that something will happen. Being in this state is how we ultimately create our experiences. Therefore, it's most likely that a "down" will follow, and when that happens, we almost sigh with relief and nod our heads, "I told you so. See, I was right!" which only reinforces the belief that caused the very situation to occur…

When something in life doesn't go our way, the most ridiculous thing to believe is that we know it all. While walking on the path of life, feeling guilty for something we did in the past, resenting others for not agreeing with us, compromising the truth for the sake of being right. . . While navigating through these powerful emotions, it would actually be ridiculous to believe that everything we know is enough and that what we experience in our lives has nothing to do with us, but really has everything to do with luck, fate, or God's will.

Knowledge can give us the tools, which in turn gives us the confidence that everything in our lives is within our power to change. We have the choice and the power to decide, even though we don't always feel that way. Whether we choose to use these valuable tools or not, what we live is only the result of our own decisions. So if you choose to live with the belief that you are not in control, you will be living a life that seems to be directed by others, yet it is really *you* who made the choice.

Have you ever considered what "What goes around comes around" really means?

This is one of the subjects I would like to touch upon outside of my music and share my perspective on it with you. Many of us think that "What goes around comes around" means that when you do bad things to anybody, you get them back in the same way. Although that is somehow true, this saying actually applies to much more. It applies to every single thought— good or bad, intention, and action that we take with regard to everything. We are building our entire existence based on "What goes around comes around".

Everything is made of energy. All material things from a pebble to a skyscraper, all our thoughts and feelings have one thing in common: energy. When we have a thought, whether it's positive or negative, whether it's well meaning, fear based, jealous or hateful, it sends out a vibration on a particular frequency. This opens us to receiving the same type of vibrations attracting people and experiences that resonate to the very frequency we hold.

"We are what we think," Buddha said. In order to be free and joyous as we were intended to be, we must focus our attention on one thing: our mind. We say "The mind wonders sometimes." We give the mind its own identity and power by believing that we have no say in what it decides to think. But we do have a say, we actually have all the say, because *we* decide. The mind is a tool— a very valuable, powerful one indeed. Nevertheless, it's a tool. That is why having free will is so meaningful. We are free to choose the kind of thoughts we want and, therefore, to live the experiences drawn to us by the strong power of our thoughts. Whether we do it consciously or by default, we are, and nobody else, shaping our reality in every single moment.

Once in a while we hear phrases that seem to be floating in the air: "It's too good to be true," or "The rich get richer, the poor get poorer." Parents, siblings, relatives, and friends try lovingly to talk you out of your "crazy" ideas, imposing their rationale or perspective. By paying attention to all that, our excitement diminishes, our emotions change, and to the degree that we give this our consent, they can put us in a state of powerlessness. Then if we take it even further and continue to entertain these negative thoughts, they slowly become new beliefs and eventually our new platform of operation.

Don't allow anything and anybody to decide what you should be thinking, how you should be feeling and therefore what you should experience in your reality. Our minds can be directed by ourselves or by others. We can truly believe in our inner voice or open our ears to others. Which do you choose? It's as simple as that.

So, next time, when you feel that your pride is hurt by somebody, when you feel guilty about something, when you feel depressed, angry, powerless, alone, discouraged, or belittled, know that you are allowing yourself to enter a state that will attract to you more of the same. Instead, the best thing you can do is make peace with where you are. Dismiss the thought that you are a victim; take responsibility for having created that very situation by having chosen the thoughts that attracted it to you. Say to yourself that it's okay where you are, and know that you can be in one hundred percent in charge of your emotions if you gently take your attention away from that which doesn't serve you. Be the firm and deliberate guardian of your thoughts— it's the *attention* we put on something that makes it so.

We possess a valuable gift: the freedom of choice. By applying it to our thoughts, we can actually decide where our life can go. Drop the heavy layers of worry, doubt, and crippling fear. Believe that it is possible and it will be. Know that you are the one who makes the decisions, and that the decisions made from the perspective of love give the most fulfilling experience of all. Operating from that standpoint will make all things possible no matter how "crazy" they may seem.

Hold onto the thought that you can achieve anything through diligent practice and do not despair when things don't come to fruition instantaneously. Relax in the knowing that each and every time you consciously and genuinely project positive thought you are actually getting a bit closer to that beautiful place where you want to be. Allow yourself to feel uplifted and empowered simply because *there is always a way*— there is no "dead end" in life.

And if you catch yourself falling, don't despair. Instead, just get up and do it all over again. How long did it take you or any of us for that matter, to get where we are? "Practice makes perfect," which is exactly what we've been doing. We've been practicing the same thought habit for years, building the foundation of both constructive and not so constructive beliefs.

Thinking negative thoughts delays the fulfillment of our desires. The good news is that thinking negative thoughts can be changed, because it is just a habit that can be broken as easily as it was created. By constant practice of focusing the mind you have the ability to break any habit no matter how strong it might be. Become consciously aware of what goes on in your mind and you will eventually have full control over the kind of thoughts you think. Remember, if you focus on negative thoughts you will attract more thoughts that don't serve you. Focus on positive thoughts, and you will attract more of them. Eventually, you will have developed a positive habit of thought. "What goes around comes around."

The mind can be an indiscriminate creator or a tool used to create. Your choice. Let it wander and it can easily create a life filled with unanswered questions. Use it as a tool, and you will intentionally create a life filled with joy and abundance. And once you come to see that you can change the way you feel by simply changing your thoughts, you will realize that nobody is in charge of your life but you. You will feel better and sure of yourself, because you know the liberating feeling of having the power to create your future experiences. You will find that the next logical step is to turn your attention to that something you considered was too late to pursue or was just a dream: your *passion*. Now reaching for your passion, reaching for your dream will be the most exciting possibility, simply because you have the confidence that it's only up to you to make it real.

Why practice your passion…? Because when we are passionate about something we feel light and happy, we have clarity and focus. Being passionate about something is one way of aligning with who we are, it's one way of aligning with God— the Source, the Inspiration. Practicing our passion connects us with All That Is and the result is always *wonder*.

Every one of us was born with a special talent. Every trade out there is somebody's creative expression. Sometimes though, finding what you are passionate about can be a problem, and I've met people who don't really know what would make their heart sing. In that case, finding your passion is the most important step. Brainstorm, try to find something you think you might enjoy doing— looking back into your childhood could help. Try to remember what made you lose track of time as a child. Pay attention to how *being* it makes you feel. Your feelings will never lie to you. If it's something that makes you feel strong, happy, and free, then you've got your answer.

However, there is one thing I would like to bring to your attention: having an open mind is crucial. What you find might come as a surprise to you, and your first impulse might not be one of acceptance. What you find might be something that now, looked at through adult eyes, might seem out of the ordinary or even impossible to achieve. THAT'S A GOOD SIGN! Dreams are called "dreams" only because they go way beyond the boundaries of what we call "possibility."

Living your passion is one way to remember the beauty and perfection of who you really are; it is one way to bring forth your true identity. I am not implying that you should give up your day job or forget about your children and your spouse while throwing yourself into a different direction. No. First, make a clear choice to love and respect yourself, and to take greater care of the inner part of yourself by making room in your schedule for that which defines you. Some might say taking time to practice what you love is selfish, but it's not. It's actually the opposite. Do what you love most and you will be serving others in the best possible way. Because practicing your passion puts you in a serene state, and from that standpoint you offer the world perfection— *your* perfection. Whatever the subject of your passion is, it is perfect because it's coming from a flawless place: your spirit.

Take that part-time course at the nearby college; start writing— if that's what gives you peace; take that once-a-week painting course you've been wishing you could attend. Making your passion part of your life, therefore living as who you really are, is the best example, gift, and inspiration you can give to your children— ever.

Once you've decided what it is you want to do, it's important to keep in mind one important detail: whatever your dream is, it's DONE. Your dream is alive and well and is waiting for you. So pursue it with great faith and patience knowing in your heart that with every ounce of happy feeling that you have, you are getting closer to it. Don't waste energy on thinking *how* it's going to happen— the Universe will take care of it. Release the resistance, appreciate where you are, and the best things will start to happen. You will be clearer, more in sync with who you are, and you will start getting brilliant ideas that will propel you toward the manifestation of your desire. Trust in what you are feeling; trust that you are capable of making the right choice. Know that feeling good is one of the most important parts of the whole process because it is a key to getting to what you want. But most of all don't let *fear* interfere with anything you do— which brings me to the next topic…

All actions that don't stem from our desire to follow our heart are to some degree based on fear. All failures and all the dreams that have never been lived have their roots in fear. But wait, what is it that actually makes one fail? Not the fear itself, but the *attention* and *importance* one places on it. The degree of failure is relative to the degree of importance we place on fear— the degree to which we lose ourselves in the nothingness of it.

We live in a society where choice based on another's expectation of us has become commonplace, making fear so deep rooted and so deceiving that it has become part of our existence. We doubt and fear that our opinions and decisions may not be good enough. We fear the unknown, we fear not finding the answer, or we fear the actual answer…

Fear confines us; it puts up a wall of illusion and blocks our innate wisdom. Before you let that happen to you, think about this: fear doesn't really exist. It's not something that we can touch or see its color. Fear is nothing but a necessary emotion we need when we lose our center. That's all that fear is. It is a signal that it's time to change the direction of our thought.

Sometimes while lost in uncertainty we ask other people for their opinions. Dismissing what you're feeling doesn't work because nobody else can know exactly what exists in your universe. Nobody can feel the way you feel with regard to anything that encompasses your life. Nobody can ever be *you* and therefore nobody can ever hear the call of your inner wisdom— your intuition.

Let's embark upon the most rewarding journey life has to offer: the journey to self-remembering. Direct your attention inward to the place where the inspiration flows in abundance, the place where you'll always find the answers perfectly tailored for you. Trust yourself. Acknowledge and celebrate who you are and where you are. Be happy with all aspects of your being. Appreciate your life; appreciate all the people in it, for they are only there to help you experience your life in the way that *you* choose. Be proud of what you've lived so far and be proud of the choices you've made and will make. Never put yourself down in front of anybody, and especially not within yourself. There is a fine line between being humble and putting yourself down.

Before we were born, we knew that God's ever-present breath would endlessly fill our sails. We knew that all we needed to do was trust and there would be no need to look back and make sure that He was there. We knew that who we are could never be apart from God. Therefore, we knew that we would have all the tools necessary to change anything we considered "negative" into something positive. In fact, we knew that we would have the power to turn our lives completely around.

We knew that destiny doesn't exist, at least not in the way

many think of it. I don't believe God would give us both free will and a set destiny. It would simply not make sense. We knew that we would have the moment of *now* as a valuable tool to create the future through our every thought and emotion. We knew there was nowhere to fall. We knew there was no other choice but for all of us to come up as winners in living life, simply because in doing so, we magnify the expression of that which is eternal— our spirit.

But most of all, we knew that the word "loser" was only a collection of letters we made up in the moment we forgot who we really were.

My Dream

Three days after I finally let go of the need to keep working on my book in an attempt to make it better, I had an unusual dream. Since I was just about to make my writings public, I felt I had a responsibility to share it with you.

A spirit, in the form of a beautiful old man, came to me in my dream and said that he had something to tell me. The next moment, I found myself in the middle of a field. "Look at this field," he said. I looked and I could see the golden beauty of a magnificent field of wheat softly humming with each touch of the gentle wind as it allowed the warmth of the sun to bathe its whole being. The old man felt my peace and tranquility. "What do you see now?" he asked. All of a sudden a storm came out of nowhere. Its strong wind was shrieking, forcing the delicate plants to bow before its powerful breath; dark clouds covered the sky, and a torrential, raging rain came down, ravaging everything in its way.

Everything was happening in 3-D around me as if I was watching a movie on a circular screen. "What do you see now?" he asked again, with a peaceful expression on his face. I felt lost, almost in pain. I was looking at this field, which in one second had been vibrating with life and, in the next second, was lying lifeless in puddles of water on the ground. "I see . . . it's dead." was all I could gasp through my frozen lips.

"Look again," the old man said gently. "In order to truly understand your meaning, you must bypass the physicality and see everything for what it really is. You understand your physical world; now you are starting to understand your spirit by opening yourself up to it, but you will truly understand your life and its purpose when you let the physicality and the spirit come together as one. You must not try to keep yourself apart from that which you can never be apart from. You must not try to keep yourself apart from Love."

"I am here to tell you that your physicality is on one side, your spirit is on the other, and all you have to do is gently push your fears away and come into the middle, where the fusing element is ready to do the work for you. Once you come into the middle and fully align with It, once you are ready to be vulnerable and trusting, to stand still with your arms wide open, with your eyes knowingly facing It, welcoming the majestic light showering down on you, once you allow Its vibration to melt the walls of sadness, grief, self-sabotage, drama, neediness, and guilt that you've built around you, once you let the unconditional Love that is in you do its work through you, then you'll truly see and understand. You will see that this field is more alive than ever before. You will see its real beauty, which is much brighter than the image your open eyes saw before the storm. You will understand that you and everything around you is eternal and can *never* die."

The moment he said that, my body started to warm from head to toe. It felt as though I had no weight, no pain, no tensions; I was free. I could feel his very presence as the embodiment of Love.

"Love" has become such a generic word. Artists, musicians and authors alike, we all try the best that we can to capture its magic through our music, writings, paintings… What we have to keep in mind is that we could never capture its feeling by intellectualizing it, by trying to find that new word, new expression or that new color to describe it without losing its simplicity and real meaning.

Now, this is what my dream helped me see, and it's a thought I would like to leave you with:

Every time we feel any kind of undesirable emotion, it only means that for a little while we have appeared to leave our center— that place of alignment where we can feel God's Love embodied as each and every one of us. The discord we sometimes feel (whether it's a simple feeling of frustration or strong despair) is nothing but our pulling away from that which WE TRULY ARE— LOVE.

Remember who you are...

and act upon it.